GOD'S POETIC WORD

This book is a treasure
That I cherish dearly
Because it reveals
Jesus Christ so clearly.

Kaye Hartley

▲ ELEVITA MEDIA

Ordering Information:
Quantity sales. Special discounts are available on quantity pur-
chases by churches and organizations. For details, contact
kaye.hartley77@gmail.com.

Printed in the United States of America

ISBN-13: 978-1494707484
ISBN-10: 1494707489

First Edition

14 13 12 11 10 / 10 9 8 7 6 5 4 3 2 1

For more information about Kaye Hartley, please visit:
www.kayehartley.com

DEDICATION

I have been writing poetry for many years, but had not considered publishing until recently. I want to dedicate this book to Wayne Cooper for opening the door to enable me to send God's Word around the world, and to my daughter, Gloria Bacon, for her support and spending so much time typing and preparing the poems.

CONTENTS

GOD

EL SHADDAI-HEBREW FOR 'THE ALMIGHTY GOD'

El Shaddai is Hebrew for the Almighty God;
He created man in His image, and said, "It's Good!"

His Name, El Shaddai, means He's more than enough
The 'All Bountiful One', Who from nothing makes stuff.

It shows He's Supplier of all our needs,
Emphasizes God's Providence, shows His mighty deeds.

Providence means foresight, control of all things;
His Nature's Immutable; He will never change.

El Shaddai planned, perfected abundance in creation,
Was manifesting the Almighty, Who has no limitation!

His Plan, from beginning, was Good for Man;
Inexhaustible resources were at His command.

The whole Plan of God for the human race
Was to shower with Love and His restorative Grace.

Grace is unmerited Favor poured out on man
For each individual who receives His Plan.

In the Word of God His Will is revealed;
He gives instructions for all our ills to be healed.

God assumes responsibility, Eternal care for His own,
Includes Provision for this life - and the one to come.

(What an AWESOME GOD! John 3:16)

EL SHADDAI: MORE THAN ENOUGH

He is El Shaddai
He's Almighty God
He's the All-Sufficient One
He's the God Who's More Than Enough.

God's more than enough
When the trials come.
He's more than enough
When everything is done.

God's more than enough
When nothing we can do.
He's more than enough
When everything's through.

God's more than enough
When we don't understand,
When all we can do
Is just hold His hand.

When the pain is so deep
No words can express;
God's more than enough
He relieves my distress.

When guilt overwhelms,
Questions: "Am I to blame?"
God's more than enough,
He eases my pain.

He whispers to me
"I look on your heart."
His gentle voice says:
"Trust Me-come apart."

So I wait in His Presence
And bow to His Throne;
He cleanses and comforts
And calls me 'His own'.

I resist the temptation
To cherish the hurt;
I must "receive" healing
As I stand on His Word.

Yes, He's more than enough
As He comforts and soothes;
The healing begins
As His love He proves.

Since I've learned to trust Him,
Through this, too, I know;
He'll not fail me now,
I'll be every whit whole.

THE CREATOR GOD

God made the seed of the flower that grows,
The scent of the lilac and the rose.

He made the trees all shades of green,
Put myriads of color on nature's screen.

God made the sky above so blue,
The white clouds that the sun peeks through.

He made the stars that shine in the night,
Gives birth to the dawn that brings new light.

He made the raindrops and the streams that flow,
The sparkling snow and the winds that blow.

God made the mountains majestically high,
It seems they're connected to the sky.

He made the oceans so wide it fills me with awe,
And the creatures within that live by His law.

God also made man; 'twas His crowing act;
That He set His love on him isn't fiction, but fact.

He made a world of beauty for him to enjoy —
With just one condition; live in God's employ.

Every blessing that God could provide for man,
Was instituted in His divine plan.

The plan "made before the foundation of the earth,"
Was followed through with Jesus Christ's birth.

He lived, loved, and died the Gospel does say,
To complete God's Plan and show us the way.

Yes, God's Only Son from the dead rose again —
And now is sitting at God's right hand.

Oh, how could I not love this Wonderful One,
Who, with all things here, gave me His Beloved Son!!!

GOD'S CREATION - FOR MAN

When God created the universe
He placed man in a world of beauty;
Endowed him with fantastic powers,
Made faith his contingent duty.

Things were living and growing for him,
All nature was clean and new;
Lovely trees of every description,
Exquisite flowers freshened by dew.

God made the birds of the air
To sing sweet songs and take flight.
They're of many shapes and colors
Which Adam could view with delight.

He formed oceans and seas so powerful
They carry ships and vessels with ease,
Sustain life great and small within them,
Provide scenes man's eyes to please.

Then there was the roof overhead;
White clouds – and all shades of blue;
With the ecstasy of the sunset
To enjoy when the day was thru.

The moon provided night light
And the stars came out to play;
Their sparkling message conveyed —
There is One ever lighting Man's way.

There's also an unseen world
He maintains for the spirit of Man;
Christ is the Door to its riches,
The fulfillment of God's divine Plan.

GOD'S LAW

What is the "Law of the Harvest"
That God created for Man—
From the beginning ordained to live by
As part of His overall Plan?

The function of this Law is –
(the order is never reversed):
For Man to receive God's Fullness,
He has to invest something first.

This unerring law is fulfilling
To the person who understands,
That this principle shows us the heart
Of the Creator Who made Man.

The investment process is simple
(It can be small or profound):
The gift of a widow's mite
Or a thousand acres of ground.

An example is the farmer,
Who plants his seed in the earth.
The seed must be buried and die
Before there's expansion and growth.

In the reaping of the harvest
It's the "single" that multiplies;
And as rain and sun work together
Resultant miracles meet the eyes.

This law not only applies
To the material aspect of life;
The One who gives God his all
Will inherit Paradise.

MY TRIUNE GOD

Jesus is my Intercessor
And that's how I know — I'm the possessor —

Of all that my Jesus bought for me
'Cause He paid the price on Calv'ry's tree.

He now sits at God's right hand-
So I can before the Father stand.

He's the High Priest Who offered His blood-
That gave me access to God's throne above.

The Holy Spirit helps me to see
All that my Jesus did for me.

The promises we claim in God's Word,
I know, deep in my spirit, it's His voice I heard.

That still, small voice I've learned to know
Who gives me assurance wherever I go.

He grows sweeter and sweeter every day;
Through His Word, the Spirit shows me the way.

My heart overflows; prayer's answered again.
I'm always amazed as His help He sends!

Thank You, Heavenly Father; Thank You, Jesus the Son,
Thank You, Holy Spirit, My God-Three in One!

I'll give You the praise as long as I'm here
For the sweet Holy Spirit Who allays my fear-

For the love of the Father, and the grace of my Lord
That gives me the vic'try through God's Word, my Sword!

OUR EARTHLY FATHER AND OUR HEAVENLY FATHER

When I think of my earthly father
The many ways he shared with me,
The times I read him a story
While sitting on his knee.

He couldn't see to read
So the order was reversed,
But my daddy knew the Bible;
He could quote many a verse.

His natural eyes were blinded
But he wasn't without hope;
For he had God's Word within him,
The Living Word that helps us cope.

There's One like an earthly father
Who always takes care of His own.
He is God, my heavenly Father
He makes my heart His throne.

The Bible says He is watching
Always conscious of my needs
And He'll surely send in abundance
Thru faith, the answer to my pleas.

A FATHER'S CARE

God is a father, Who cares for His own.
We're instructed to pray to Him on His throne.
But He's not far away; He's always near.
We're told that He sees each falling tear.

His promise is to always be true.
He'll be there even when troubles ensue.
He'll make every hardship quicken our pace.
They'll turn to blessings, bring joy to our face.

If you'll walk with Him and trust Him, you'll see.
Demons choose to enslave; but God'll set free.
So thank God for the trial, and His Word
That says, "All things work together for good".

And the child of God who truly believes
Is the one who, by faith, really sees
That the answer comes first on His heart screen;
He knows it's received before it is seen.

GOD'S LOVE IS SO POWERFUL

God loves you!
He's very real.

He wants you to know
He cares how you feel.

Just bow your head,
Ask Christ in your heart;

New life to you
He'll surely impart.

He'll change your life,
Give you new hope.

With His guidance
He'll help you to cope

With the cares of life
That have overwhelmed;

And things will change
With Christ at the helm.

So take that first step,
Trust God and you'll see:

His power in your life
Will set you free.

Give Him full reign
To chart your course;

The power of prayer
Is a mighty force.

GOD LOVES YOU

God's love is abiding
And you can be sure
He'll continue to bless you
For His Word does endure.

His promises cover
Every need of man
And what you need now
Is contained in His Plan.

So look for a scripture,
Specific and true;
By faith stake your claim
And He'll give it to you.

GOD KNOWS – HE CARES

God knows when you're heavy-hearted,
He knows when your heart is sore;
God knows when the way grows weary,
He knows when you can take 'no more'.

God knows when you are so lonely,
He knows when the road seems so long-
God knows when friends have failed you,
He knows when you've lost your song.

God knows all about you – still loves you,
He loves you when you're right or wrong;
God sent Jesus to die for your sins,
So, adopted in His family, you'll belong.

Jesus is closer than a brother,
He wants all your burdens to share;
Jesus knows what you are "going thru",
He knows because He has "been there".

So, open your heart to this Savior,
Pray! Ask Him in your heart to abide;
He'll make you a new creation,
As your friend, always walk by your side.

Then – when life on Earth is over,

And you hear God say: "Time is no more;"

A home in Heaven will be awaiting you,

For Jesus said: "I am the door".

GOD IN US – HIS DWELLING PLACE

The God of Miracles
Dwells within my heart,
He is the same as-
He was-at the start.

Where is His Temple?
I am His dwelling place!
I commune with Him
And experience His grace.

Jesus told His People
He'd return to His Father,
But — He'd come again —
They should "wait" together.

They obeyed His instruction
In the Upper Room;
The Holy Spirit fell-
They were all transformed!

When the Spirit came-
Made Christ's Presence real,
He promised never to leave —
Jesus' Word He'd fulfill.

He's our Comforter, Guide.
His purpose: to indwell.
He's our constant companion,
He does "all things well."

He is very real,
He's with me to lead;
He gives me wisdom
In time of need.

He opens my eyes –
Divine love captures me
With intimate knowledge
Proved on Calvary's tree.

I know in my heart
Every longing Christ meets;
He's waiting for me
At the "Mercy Seat."

The 'Spirit of Prayer'
Takes me to God's throne;
Jesus, the High Priest,
Shows me what He has done.

Jesus Christ was the altar-
And…The Sacrifice,
The price of my soul
He did suffice!

He's the Justice of God,
My righteousness.
I can call God "Father",
I'm not cursed-but blessed!

I have a "New Covenant",
Purchased by Blood;
I'm a child of the King,
I can ask for all "Good".

God wills this for me,
I agree with my Father.
His promise to me:
"Everything I'll recover."

This is Jubilee's year,
The Church's finest hour.
God's people set free
We're moving into His power.

Let's pray God's promises
Saturate our heart,
Crush Satan's plans,
Tear his kingdom apart.

Meditate on God's Word,
Our spirits filled with Praise,
Boldness will arise
God's Banner we'll raise.

The Word performs Itself,
His Word is "in Power",
Let's accept nothing less-
This is our greatest hour.

It is not time to say-
I will not let it slip;
I'm giving God control!
Let Him pilot my ship.

Christ said, "It is finished!"
(The enemy's defeated).
The Lord is in heaven
With His Father seated.

Our fight's the good fight!
Faith is our shield.
We will stand on God's Word-
And never yield!

By Faith we can See
The answer is here.
Let's believe "It is done."
There's no need to fear.

So…for our Miracle today
Have Expectation.
Receive the Answer – by Faith.
And – accept no exception!

YOU ARE LOVED

You are in my thoughts today,
I hold you up to God, and pray.

Even though the way seems steep,
God answers prayer; He will you keep.

And though to God you can't reach out,
You can't see God; you're filled with doubt.

He still is there upon His throne;
His Word is sure- the work is done.

He'll meet your need and make you sure,
His promise will for e'er endure.

His love is strong, it'll pass the test.
When you can't understand, He'll still give rest.

So be assured you're not alone,
I'm taking you to Christ, God's Son.

I love you with a love divine,
As though you were a child of mine.

So any time of night or day,
If I can help along the way,

Please let me know – what-e're the need,
Know someone's there your voice to heed!

If you don't want to lend an ear,
You just want someone to be near,

We'll share a meal and fellowship,
Or, if you want, we'll take a trip.

I hope I've made my message clear:
To God and me – you're very dear.

SOMEONE CARES – GOD AND I

I thought of you this morning
As I knelt before the Lord:
I asked Him to be with you,
Speak peace thru His Word.

As I waited in His Presence,
Sent His love on wings of prayer;
I knew He drew you to Him,
Gently eased away your care.

You must keep your eyes on Jesus.
He's the Author of your faith.
He's the One Who gives vict'ry.
He's the One Who sets the pace.

We must prepare for the conflict;
The "Battle of the Mind";
Be surrounded by God's forces,
To the enemy – "not blind".

The Battle is the Lord's!
It's been "fought and won" for us.
So claim it – stand your ground;
And in the Lord – Rejoice!

GOD BLESS YOU

May God be very near you
May you know His healing touch:

Be assured that we are praying
And we love you very much.

GOD'S AMAZING LOVE

When love overflows
It is divine;
It amazes me –
That God's love is mine.

It's mine to receive,
And to enjoy –
To realize always
It's mine to employ.

This love is powerful!
As I receive,
It flows through me,
And others Believe.

Love flows only
When channels are clear;
It reaches out –
To those who are dear.

When love flows out,
It goes far and near;
Because it's active –
And always spreads cheer.

The love of God,
His love Divine –
Must flow through me
To remain mine.

And as it flows –
To Man who's the course;
It's love that's supreme
And Christ is the Source.

For love to be real
Submission's the key;
When I'm filled with God –
He flows through me!

GOD NEVER FAILS

It is so hard to put in words
The way you really feel;

Especially at a time like this
When life just seems to reel.

But thru it all I hear God's voice
Saying to me in His Word;

"If you will put your trust in Me
I'll work it for your good."

So I'll have faith in God always,
Wherever life's road leads.

For He has never failed me yet,
He's pledged to meet my needs.

GOD'S OPEN HEAVEN

God prepared a place
For our Loved One to rest;

A cocoon of comfort -
Where His Presence blessed.

There was quiet and peace,
As we worshipped and prayed;

There was no hurt nor pain;
All our fears were allayed.

All was one accord -
Our Love made her secure;

As we said, "Good bye" -
Of this, we were sure.

Then the Angels came,
They were God's provision;

In Jesus' Name! They-
Ushered her into heaven.

JESUS, A TRUE FRIEND

Jesus is a friend that sticks closer than a brother.
He is always there when there is no other.

He's a true friend on Whom you can depend.
He's the Alpha and Omega; the Beginning and the End.

Jesus Christ is the One by Whom all things consist;
Yet nothing is too small to ask Him to assist.

He walks with me every moment of the day;
He's never too busy to show me the way.

He gives Peace, Joy, Fulfillment as I let Him lead;
I'm sure He's trustworthy-and He knows my every need.

The secret of contentment is in making His will mine;
As I learn to do this, life is filled with more sunshine.

He will go with me when Eternity I face
Because He's the author of time and space.

He bridged the gulf between Heaven and Hell;
And I know when life is over – with my soul - it's well.

Jesus gave His life for me – has love beyond compare.
He died to give me life on Earth and Heaven with me share.

JESUS, MY ALL

I'm so in love with Jesus;
I'm glad I am His own.
He sees my every weakness
Though to others they're unknown.

God's Word says that He loved me
Though my life was steeped in sin;
When I asked Him to forgive me,
He came to dwell within.

Now I'm overwhelmed with wonder;
It's such a thrill to know
That Jesus is a Friend to me,
Is mine where'ere I go.

He's my teacher and instructor;
His Spirit helps me grow.
His Blood's a cleansing agent
That's a never-ending flow.

He's my source of confidence;
The leveler of my life.
He makes His Presence known to me,
Helps me to cope with strife.

He walks with me in valleys
As well as mountain heights.
Whatever route my path does take
He makes things come out right.

THE BENEFITS OF CALVARY

God's Spirit speaks to me
Of a long ago scene

As I ponder what I see
What does this suffering mean?

God's Son came to redeem
From the bondage where we've been —

The great price He paid for me
Was death on Calvary's tree.

He washed my sins away
From sin and sickness set me free —

Oh, praise the name of Jesus
For the blood He shed for me.

ON CALVARY

It is done, the work is done;
It was completed by the Son.
The work was done for me
On Calvary.

It is done, the work is done;
"It is finished," cried the Son.
Praise God! Redemption's won
On Calvary.

"It is finished," Jesus said.
The proof: He rose from the dead
After His blood was shed
On Calvary.

NEW LIFE IN CHRIST

Springtime's a wonderful
Time of the year.
Winter is over –
And summer is near.

Flowers peek their heads
Through the warm earth;
They show us everywhere
Nature's new birth.

When we think of new life,
The bud and the bloom –
We know Christ's our Source,
In our hearts He must have room.

He brings fragrance and beauty,
Lights with myriad hues;
He is the Resurrection!-
To the life He renews.

John 3:16
For God so loved the world that He gave His only begotten Son, that
whoever believes in Him should not perish but have everlasting life.
Romans 10:9,10
 That if you confess with your mouth the Lord Jesus and believe in your
heart that God has raised Him from the dead, you will be saved.

THE HOLY SPIRIT

The precious Holy Spirit
Is a gift from the Lord.
He came as Jesus promised
In fulfillment of His Word.

He's a member of the Godhead;
He's very God in power.
He is a real Person;
Makes Christ live in us each hour.

In the Old Testament
His coming was foretold.
When Jesus went to Heaven
He sent the Spirit to the world.

He is called 'the Comforter'
Was sent in Jesus' name.
Jesus said He'd teach us "all things"
He assures us Christ's the same.

The Spirit has no limits —
He has access to God's throne;
He'll lead us safely in this world,
Escort us to our heavenly home.

GOD'S WORD

GOD'S WORD: SURE, DEPENDABLE

God's Word is His bond
And will stand forevermore;

It's the very breath and life
Of our God – our Creator.

It's not just the written word,
A page contained in a book;

It's the Person who is God,
Revealed by His Son's work.

The Word that God speaks
Is alive and full of power,

The very Son of God
Imparting life every hour.

It's active and operative
Energizing and effective.

It's sharper than a sword
Correcting everything defective;

It can penetrate, divide
The soul and the spirit,

The deepest part of our nature
Can analyze and "sift it".

God's Word can expose,
Judge our thoughts, right or wrong,

Show the purpose of the heart
Place deep within – a song.

Oh, let us not sell short
The power of "The Word";

Because in very essence
It's the incarnate Son of God.

It's the Holy Spirit's work
To reproduce in us,

All that God's Word commands
So His children He can bless.

So let's trust the Holy Spirit,
Depend upon His power—

To make God's Word alive
And active in us each hour.

GOD'S WORD, A SEED

God's Word is a seed
I must plant in my heart.
It'll meet every need
If I give it a start.

It'll perform what it says
If I sow it each day,
Tho in reaping, at times
There may be a delay.

But the Word of His promise
Is steadfast and sure.
I know it'll happen
If I but endure.

The testing that comes-
The trial to my faith,
Will help make me strong
If I patiently wait.

God's Word has been proven
By many a saint.
This foundation's my claim,
I'll trust and not faint.

I thank God, my Lord,
For His promises true;
And I give you my word,
He'll never fail you!

GOD'S MESSAGE – IN HIS WORD

God gave me a message to give you:
He said if you'll believe His Word,
He'll do great and mighty things for you –
Such as you've never seen or heard.

His greatest desire is to bless you;
To provide you with all you need.
But His blessings come with His Presence,
And His voice He wants you to heed.

So go to God's Word; search the Scriptures.
Mine the silver, the gold, precious stones.
Take the promise the Spirit gives you.
Trust His Word; claim it for your own.

Let nothing, or no one deter you,
Determine in your heart to go through.
God promises to always be with you.
He'll not fail you; He'll prove His Word true.

Meditate on the promise in Scripture
That you are praying God will fulfill.
Faith will be produced in your heart
And you'll be assured God's Word – is His Will!

Also, praise and thank God in your heart;
For when you think on His Word – faith grows!
Expectation will make it happen,
The answer comes to the heart – that knows!

THE POWERFUL WORD

(Hebrews 4:12; Proverbs 17:17; I Thessalonians 2:13)

God's Word is omnipotent,
It has creative power;

It can bring into existence
What it speaks – each day or hour.

From the living God comes life
Through the living Word;

It's creative, quickening power;
Is released by faith in God.

The Word will work in me
What it promises, commands;

His voice is in power
We're secure in God's hands.

JESUS CHRIST, THE WORD

This Book of life
Has its origin in Heaven,

Let it be your guide
Right direction you'll be given.

For the Word is a Person
Jesus Christ is His name

To show us the Father
Is the reason He came.

So read Psalm Thirty Seven
And One Hundred Nineteen.

Turn to Saint John One One
And Jesus Christ will be seen.

The promises are there
Every one is to you.

The Spirit of God
By faith makes them come true.

THE GIFT GOD'S WORD

This gift that I bring
Is a favorite of mine.

It's the Book more precious
Than all verse or rhyme.

It can change your life
From mediocre to sublime

Remove clouds of doubt
Bring Christ's light divine.

So whatever life brings
Whether friend or foe,

Know Someone is speaking —
His voice you will know.

His Word is His promise
And it makes your faith grow.

THE BEST GIFT, THE BIBLE

This gift is the best
That a person could give;
Its words contain life
Shows us how to live.

If I had great wealth,
A legacy to leave,
The most valuable thing
Anyone could receive,

I'd still put this Book
At the top of the list;
If you read it each day,
Your life it'll bless.

A PROMISE OF DAILY GUIDANCE

God dropped a piece of insight
Into my heart today.
He promised to instruct me
And teach me in the way.

He said that He'd take charge,
Provide my needs today –
He'd guide me with His eye
If I'd just take time to pray.

The treasured little nugget
That He dropped into my heart,
Is a simple daily plan
Of which He would be a part.

God, Himself, is our example
With His everlasting Plan;
He's written us a memo- (His Word)
Telling of His love for Man.

He gave written instructions,
And His Spirit speaks each day:
To the one who's mind is open
He will teach and show the way.

So with this divine example,
When I plan my day and ask –
God will bring success and blessing
And help with every task.

Psalm 32:8
"I will instruct thee and teach thee in the way which thou shalt go: I will guide thee with mine eye."
(KJV)

THE CREATIVE POWER OF GOD'S WORD IN MY MOUTH

God created everything in heaven and earth,
Things of great value, and those of small worth.

God's Word contains His creative power;
It's alive! full of life, every day, each hour.

We are made in His image, and we must speak-
To receive, specifically, the things we seek.

The Word of His power produced what He spoke;
I'm part of His Body; I'm in His yoke.

When God's creative Word is within me-
The things I say produce things I can see.

Therefore, what I believe I must confess-
That I may God's gifts really possess.

As I speak God's Word from my heart –
The Holy Spirit does faith impart.

The power of God's spoken Word
Must come from my mouth, can be heard –

In order for God to bring it to pass,
And perform for me what I ask.

It must resound in heaven and earth
For the seed in my heart to come to birth.

My mouth is the instrument God does use,
So – God's Word, in my mouth, I must choose.

The first day of Creation – God spoke!
The light came – the whole world awoke!

For the darkness around us to be shattered anew,
The Light of God's Presence – in our lives – must burst
through.

His Word comes to Life in us – as His Spirit reveals…
The Light of God's Son – Whom the darkness repeals.

GOD'S OMNIPOTENT WORD

God's Word is food for my soul;
Its constant diet makes me whole

Whatever I need it does supply;
Its great beauty attracts my eye.

The more I feed on this wonderful food
I want to share it – it is so good!

How sweet are your words to my taste;
They're pure and holy – there is no waste.

*This Word is sweeter than honey to me;
It helps me become what God wants me to be.

There's power to do everything – in HIS Word
In it are the sweetest sounds ever heard.

*This Word is a Person, Jesus Christ, God's Son
It's His power that can get anything done.

*He is also called, "the Bread of Life";
He feeds my spirit – makes things come out right.

This spiritual nutrition keeps me healthy and strong
It's also there when things seem to go wrong.

*It's more than adequate when I need to be healed –
By Jesus, my Savior, my redemption is sealed.

*Psalms 119:103
*Hebrews 1:3
*John 6:35
*Psalms 107:20

CHRIST, THE WORD

The Word of God is quick and sure
It everlastingly will endure:

Upon this Rock I am secure
For all life's ills, Christ is the cure.

THE LIVING WORD

For life and health and happiness
I must each day be fed.

The Word of God fulfills my need
It's Christ, the Living Bread.

PSALM 119:89; ISAIAH 40:8

The Word of God
Is settled in Heaven;
It's the Book of the ages
It'll stand forever.

Psalm 119:89 "Forever, O LORD,
Your word is settled in heaven."

Isaiah 40:8 "The grass withers, the flower fades,
But the word of our God stands forever."

PSALM 119:105

Cherish this Word; it's a lamp
It is Jesus, who'll show you the way.

Love this Word; it's a light
It illumines, turns night into day.

Psalm 119:105 "Your word *is* a lamp to my feet
And a light to my path."

DEUTERONOMY 8:3; II TIMOTHY 3:16

By bread alone Man does not live
But by every Word that God does give.

All Scripture is given by God's inspiration
It's profitable to us and gives instruction.

Deut. 8:3 "So He humbled you, allowed you to hunger, and fed you with manna which you did not know nor did your fathers know, that He might make you know that man shall not live by bread alone; but man lives by every word that proceeds from the mouth of the LORD."

II Timothy 3:16 "All Scripture is given by inspiration of God, and is profitable for doctrine, for reproof, for correction, for instruction in righteousness,"

I PETER 1:25

The Word of God is very sure
We know it will for'er endure;
Upon God's Word we can depend
Of its power there is no end.

I Peter 1:25 "But the word of the LORD endures forever."

PRAYER

MORNING PRAYER

Upon first consciousness of morn
I want to God with praise adorn.

My first thought, and my last one, too
I want to give, dear Father, to you.

I want to nurture our relationship
And promote a closer fellowship.

The need, so great, is truly mine
To have your love upon me shine.

I cannot cope this day with care
Unless I spend time first in prayer.

It makes me know your love and will;
I know good comes from You, no ill.

I need not fear; You're in control
To pray and follow You is my role.

It's only time spent with You there
That gives me confidence elsewhere.

I know on You I can depend;
From all evil You'll defend.

Oh, what a blessed place to bow,
Renew my faith and pay my vow.

As I awake, and in my head
I bow my heart upon my bed.

THE NEED OF PRAYER

Prayer's an essential law of God,
The material that holds life together;
It creates the atmosphere needed for us
To grasp the treasures of Heaven.

Moses' knowledge of God was intimate;
But still the need was not lessened –
To spend time with the Sovereign of Heaven,
Who was his Source of life's essence.

This closeness brought clearer insight
Into the need and nature of prayer,
As before the throne of His Majesty,
He silently waited there.

He was led to see greater indebtedness,
Pray and discover the larger results;
In the crisis of a nation's existence
Said, "I fell down before the Lord".

The whole of Bible purpose
Is to produce faith and make us aware –
That in the final analyses
The cohesion of life is through prayer.

To God, prayer's the only access –
To secure His favor, the only means;
If we want to affect the Father,
We must do it on our knees.

He has given us many promises.
We may know Him; receive what we need,
But now, as at the beginning,
There are conditions we must heed.

There's an enemy in the universe
That would use every means and power
To keep us from the knowledge and practice
Of prayer for even one hour.

He blinds man to the need of obedience
And the access that God did intend,
Stacks up circumstances against him
And then, stands by to condemn.

In prayer we find all the answers
To difficulties, problems and such;
It's the vehicle that bears our petitions
To our Father who loves us so much.

Prayer's the channel from which all good flows
From God to man, and then on
From man to each life he touches;
Becomes incense before God's throne.

Prayer enhances man's ability to reason,
Elevates, enlarges, uplifts,
It becomes the school of wisdom;
Replaces unsteady sand that shifts.

Prayer brings unlimited possibilities
To the one who'll make the investment.
Precious time spent in God's Presence
Gives power to make life's adjustments.

Revelation mends relationships.
It is brought about through prayer.
By it we understand principles;
Our duties are also made clear.

By the faith that prayer develops,
A process of growth takes place.
In this life shines the Glory of Jesus
And others come to know His Grace.

PRAYER AND GOD'S GRACE

God is making real to me
The wonders of His grace
As I bow my heart before Him,
He shows His precious face.

When I wait in humble silence,
The Spirit works within,
And there comes a sweet assurance
He has answered prayer again.

Oh, the wonder of the grace of God!
I cannot understand
How the Maker of the universe
Could give His son to man.

Yet, as I tarry longer
In the presence of the Lord,
His Spirit whispers to my heart,
"The answer's in My Word."

It's found in Saint John, chapter three:
For God so loved the world
He sent His only son to die,
So fellowship's restored.

The need for this is written
In the record of Beginnings.
When the first man, Adam, failed the test,
That started man to sinning.

So God in loving forethought
Had authored a Plan
Whereby Christ, the holy, sinless One
Could substitute for man.

Though now I see the cause of sin,
The need for help, a Savior,
My finite mind can't comprehend
God's unmerited favor.

For that is what the word "grace" means
(It's Webster's definition).
But the deeper meaning needs to grip
My heart and bring contrition.

This is where the power of prayer
Brings answers to petition;
It is the grace of God that brings
Our praying to fruition.

It's the Spirit's intercession
That brings answers, and His power.
There's nothing I can do or be
But yield to Him that hour.

For prayer's the only power
That can open Heaven to me;
And God's unmerited favor
Is what turns the key.

So in the presence of the Lord
I will stay, I'll wait;
And allow His matchless grace
To turn the key to Heaven's gate.

INTERCESSION

As is in the presence of the Lord
I sat and thought upon His Word
The Spirit impressed upon my heart
Someone's need to bring to God.

I held that one to God in prayer
And then, as I felt eased,
I waited for His voice to speak;
Direct me as He pleased.

There came a strong desire within
To understand the message;
Receive the insight that prayer brings,
The Holy Spirit blessing.

For, as I prayed and lingered there,
I visualized a cross.
Hanging on it was God's own Son;
On Him, our debt. What cost!!

I thought of how he suffered
As stripes on Him were laid.
The picture was so vivid
I could not turn my gaze.

In the stripes I saw the blood,
The blood that flowed from God!
The Word says "By His stripes we're healed",
And the question came, "Why, Lord?"

The Spirit sent me to the Word.
At first there came no sight;
But, as I persevered and searched,
A reference brought the light.

Sickness came because of sin.
For sin there must be judgment.
Stripes were the instruments that brought
Healing in atonement.

So by the blood, from stripes, that flowed
Our redemption's been completed.
And the terrible debt that sin incurred
Is a debt that's now deleted.

Now all that remains for the answer
Is only one thing more.
God's done all that He can do;
He sent Christ Who is the door.

You must have faith in God's Son.
His work is done, complete.
His commandment is, "Ask what you will."
Stand firm! Don't accept defeat.

Praise God! for His blessings and count it as done.
His Word and prayer are the key.
Say, "I'll bless the Lord with all my heart
For His abundant provisions for me."

INTERCESSION: FOR MY PASTOR'S WIFE

I saw in my vision my fellow minister's wife –
How she struggled under the load she carried that night.

The burden was not grievous that she took – it was right
But it got heavier as her strength seemed to take flight.

As I watched the Lord appeared at her side,
Took the burden-attached a yoke – and she kept stride.

She regained her strength as she walked thru the night –
The way became brighter – as she walked in His Light.

The infusion of strength was – the Blessings of His Presence,
And the peace of the Lord – revealed His omnipotence.

She was refreshed – on the road that she trod
Because . . . with great wonder . . .

She was walking with God! "El Shaddai".

PRAYER IS THE KEY

There is an invisible world
It's real-even though it's unseen;
The Kingdom of God is in man
Though not yet on the visible scene.

God sent His Son to the world
That the world might be saved from sin
Jesus Christ, the image of God
Came to reconcile God and men.

He came in the form of man
A babe in a manger so low;
He grew and experienced all things
So life on earth He could know.

The reason God's Son did this:
Took the robe of flesh as His own
Was to open the door of heaven
To all men make its riches known.

He came to reveal God's Kingdom
To set up His rule – and reign
In the heart of all mankind
To give us power in His name.

Yes, the Kingdom of God is here now,
The only entrance is by revelation;
The Holy Spirit opens our hearts
Christ, as Savior, works our transformation.

Then all God's Word – His Promises
Become ours as we study and pray:
For prayer is the Key to God's secrets
And obedience to His Word shows the way.

Jesus said, "I am the Door."
He said, "I'm the Truth, the Way."
John's Gospel says Christ is God's Word.
So listen to what God has to say.

PRAYER PARTNER

A prayer partner shares
Your needs and concerns;
Another's burden you bear
As for souls you yearn.

There's help when discouraged.
In God's Word we're told:
"Agree" in prayer;*
To "obey" makes us bold.*

We must pray every day:
Be faithful and true.
When the answer's delayed,
Persevere. "Pray through".

This covenant's of value,
Is one of great worth;
It reaches "the Sovereign"
Of heaven and earth.

It covers all "promises"
Found in God's Word.
His "store's" without limit
When Christ is our "Lord".

Each request is a goal
That "by faith" we attain;
The Holy Spirit's our Guide
As we pray "in Christ's Name".

When we pray for others,
God's love shines through.
You, also, reap blessings:
Others praying for you.

GOD ANSWERS PRAYER!

*Matthew 18:19
*Galations 6:9

A PASSION FOR SOULS

Lord, place within me the passion for souls
That is the prerequisite to win —
Those who are lost without hope in this world
Without Christ, will reap hell for their sins.

Oh, God, give me a concern that'll take
Me to the closet of prayer,
And give me the leading of your Spirit to know
The one whose heart you've prepared.

Then give me the love only you can give
That'll be sensitive, fearless, yet kind;
Love that'll "hold on" and never let go
That in nothing falls behind.

Let me be that channel connected to you
That one thru whom your life flows.
Let the Holy Spirit set my heart aflame
With a fire of zeal that glows.

Let my life be invested in precious stock
Whose quality's never diminished;
May many souls come to know my Lord
And share eternity when this life is finished.

PRAYER FOR SOULS

O God, give me a burden
For souls lost in sin;
Help me to work and pray
That you'll save and cleanse within.

The harvest field is white
There's no hope for souls I meet,
For those whom my life touches
'Til I work and pray and weep.

As I give my life anew
To labor in your field,
I know Your Spirit leads
To those He'll cause to yield.

Thank you, God, for Your assurance
That in answer to my prayer —
Your Word gives me the promise
That they'll heaven with me share.

REVIVAL

Revival's not free; it's a costly thing.
We can't just pray at church and sing.
It takes commitment to God and man—
Unceasing prayers to fulfill His Plan.

It's the morning watch when first awake
God wants from us, and then He'll take
Into account, throughout the day,
The other times we pause to pray.

Communication with God is prayer;
It's lifting our heart to Him everywhere.
The access door is always ajar;
We oil its hinges in the morning hour.

When we give God firstfruit of our time,
We're blest as we walk with Him, not blind
To the whitened harvest field we're in,
The souls in our world, lost in sin.

We'll surely see many lives transformed;
When the Christian's revived, souls are reborn.
For Revival comes to the Church as she sees
God responds to a people who are on their knees.

EMPATHY

You were in my thoughts on this special day.
My heart longed to reach out to you.
I was hindered from making contact;
But God assured me my prayers got through.

So I lifted you up to the Father
With whom there's no distance or space.
Through my prayer for you I was comforted;
I knew you'd experience God's grace.

Not only was God watching over you,
He gave you favor of others around.
He makes "all things work together for good"
Because His love for you abounds.

He can take any circumstance of life
And keep it from causing us harm.
If the power of faith is persisted in
There need be no cause for alarm.

So, you see, God overruled the bad
That was meant to incapacitate you.
He'll continue to fight your battles;
Bring vict'ry for you all the way through.

So trust Him to do the impossible!
He delights in blessing His own.
He has the means and the power to do so.
He'll never, never leave you alone.

HEAVENLY RADAR

God is a present help
In time of trouble.
He's a God who's near
And never far.

God heals all sickness
He's the One who answers
Prayers we pray in faith
Wher-e're we are.

So trustfully rest
And claim His promises
Receive the answer
Heaven's door's ajar.

So many people
Have been praying for you
Faith's answer comes by route
Of heavenly radar.

MOM'S PRAYER
(after daughter's miscarriage)

Thank you, God for my child, so precious is she:
Minister to her need and thus bless me.

Be very real to her in this trying hour,
In the loss of that little life before it could flower.

Hold her close, let her head lean on your breast:
Enfold her in Your arms and give her rest.

Let her know that little lamb is in Your care:
It was – and is – Your precious Jewel, so fair.

May she understand that as she loved, yet never saw
Her kinship with You strengthens, yet there's awe.

Be there the times her arms feel empty, ache
And for the absent one her longing heart would break.

Reveal Your Son with healing in His wings.
Let Your love flow through a human heart that sings

Of the Grace of God that lets His loved one share
Love not fulfilled, and yet beyond compare,

And thus begin to know in some small measure,
The greatness of God's gift, His Son: What treasure!!

Thank you, God, for blessing my child: she's Yours too.
You promised to care for Your own, and Your Word is true.

I'M PRAYING FOR YOU

I'm praying God will bless you
And keep you in His care.

I'm sending you this greeting
Trust that it will bring you cheer.

PRAYER PERSPECTIVE

Go to the Lord
Wait in His Presence.

Take your request
Hang it on a Promise.

Believe it will happen
Praise God it is done.

The peace of God comes
And the victry's won.

MY PRAYER FOR BELOVED TRAVELERS

May the Lord watch over and keep you
As you travel on your way.

May His Presence be with you
Every moment of the day.

May His angels go before you,
Keep you safe from all harm.

May your travel be pleasant
With no cause for alarm.

May your fellowship be sweet
As your acquaintance you renew;

And the Holy spirit visit you
With blessings, not a few.

May God's grace be upon you
As you travel every mile

And may you uplift one another
With good humor and a smile.

May God's Presence that's within you
Flow out to bring sweet peace,

May you enjoy the conference
And bless others that you meet.

My prayer as you journey:
"God will bring you back refreshed

Fill your hearts with joy –
And bring you safely home to rest."

PRAYER: GOD BLESS AMERICA

Dear God, Bless America
The red, white and blue;
The land that you provided
For man to worship you.

To worship you in freedom
And liberty in the Spirit;
To build a Godly country
Through our lives we'll help you fill it.

Fill this land of plenty
With the blessings you intended —
When you led the man, Columbus,
To explore – gave him incentive.

May the colors of our flag
And their meaning be revealed;
Red, the blood of Jesus
Saves – and by His stripes we're healed.

The cleansing of the sinner
Is denoted by the white,
The cross of Jesus Christ
Turns a life around – makes right.

Blue, the heavenly color
Gives the promise of tomorrow.
God's Word – true, eternal
Takes care of every sorrow.

The colors of my country
Are God's kingdom colors, too.
As children of His Kingdom,
Abundant blessings come to you.

PRAYER, A GIFT

The sweetest words:
"I'll pray for you" –
A priceless gift,
Forever new.

Such a peace!
Each day to know
You bear my name-
Before the Throne.

What a comfort!
Se-cur-i-ty!!
To "rest" upon
Your prayer for me.

ABOUT THE AUTHOR

K aye Hartley was born and raised in a small town in Ohio. She attended Bible college in Kentucky where she met her husband, Reverend O. Joe Hartley. Upon graduation, the young couple was asked by the Ohio District of the Assemblies of God to start a new church in Portsmouth, OH. And off they went.

From there they were asked to pastor a new Assembly of God

church in the small town of Hicksville, Ohio, where they stayed for three years. Following their work in Hicksville, they moved to Fort Wayne, IN, where they were invited to plant another A/G church. They also pastored churches in Cleveland, OH and Springfield, OH, and traveled throughout the midwestern and southern states ministering and preaching the gospel.

Their last church start-up was located near Charlotte, NC. It was during the initial stages of building that ministry that Kaye's husband of 44 years went to be with the Lord he served so faithfully.

During all those years of ministry, in addition to raising a family of three children, Kaye was her husband's associate. She shared teaching, and preaching responsibilities as well as doing most of the counseling and mentoring.

Due to her varied experience and keen knowledge of the Word, she was often the speaker for local and state women's ministry functions, as well as being active as a sectional director of women's ministries.

Since her husband's death, she has been active teaching, mentoring, and counseling as the opportunities arise.

Kaye continues to write poetry and other inspirational writings. You can visit her at: kayehartley.com

POSTSCRIPT

Everyone is going to die one day. God loves you and wants you to know Him. If you have any questions concerning where you will spend eternity, or how to be prepared to meet God and be ready for heaven, or if you just want prayer – you may contact me at kaye.hartley77@gmail.com.

To accept Christ into your life as your Savior, go to the Bible and read:

John 3:16 [16] For God so loved the world that He gave His only begotten Son, that whoever believes in Him should not perish but have everlasting life.

Romans 3:23 [23] for all have sinned and fall short of the glory of God,

Romans 6:23 [23] For the wages of sin is death, but the gift of God is eternal life in Christ Jesus our Lord.

Romans 5:12-21 [12] Therefore, just as through one man sin entered the world, and death through sin, and thus death spread to all men, because all sinned — [13] (For until the law sin was in the world, but sin is not imputed when there is no law. [14] Nevertheless death reigned from Adam to Moses, even over those who had not sinned according to the likeness of the transgression of Adam, who is a type of Him who was to come. [15] But the free gift is not like the offense. For if by the one man's offense many died, much more the grace of God and the gift by the grace of the one Man, Jesus Christ, abounded to many. [16] And the gift is not like that which came through the one who sinned. For the judgment which came from one offense resulted in condemnation, but the free gift which came from many offenses resulted in justification. [17] For if by the one man's offense death reigned through the one, much more those who receive abundance of grace and of the gift of righteousness will reign in life through the One, Jesus Christ.)

[18] Therefore, as through one man's offense judgment came to all men, resulting in condemnation, even so through one Man's righteous act the free gift came to all men, resulting in justification of life. [19] For as by one man's disobedience many were made sinners, so also by one Man's obedience many will be made righteous.

[20] Moreover the law entered that the offense might abound. But where sin abounded, grace abounded much more, [21] so that as sin reigned in death, even so grace might reign through righteousness to eternal life through Jesus Christ our Lord.

Romans 10:9-13   [9] that if you confess with your mouth the Lord Jesus and believe in your heart that God has raised Him from the dead, you will be saved. [10] For with the heart one believes unto righteousness, and with the mouth confession is made unto salvation. [11] For the Scripture says, "Whoever believes on Him will not be put to shame."[a] [12] For there is no distinction between Jew and Greek, for the same Lord over all is rich to all who call upon Him. [13] For "whoever calls on the name of the LORD shall be saved."[b]

PRAYER

Dear Heavenly Father,
I know I am a sinner, and I ask for your forgiveness. I believe your
son, Jesus, died for my sins and rose from the dead. I trust and follow
Him as my Lord and Savior. Guide my life and help me to do your
will.
In Jesus' name, amen.

If you prayed this prayer and would like to know more, contact
me at kaye.hartley77@gmail.com

Recommended Books

WritersInTheSpirit.com

KayeHartley.com

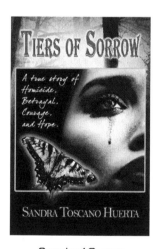

Sandra4G.com

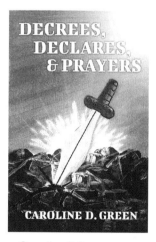

CarolineDGreen.com

26896314R00070

Made in the USA
Charleston, SC
23 February 2014